# Six Principles of British Nationalism

## by

## John Tyndall

**The A.K. Chesterton Trust**

**2012**

Originally published in 1966 by Albion Press. Second edition 1970, Albion Press.

This edition is *The A.K. Chesterton Trust Reprint Series* No. 7.

Printed & Published in 2012.

**ISBN:** 978-0-9564669-7-6

This edition is dedicated to the memory of its author, John Tyndall.

# Foreword to this edition

Although in some regards rather dated, we have great pleasure in reprinting this important ideological work on British Nationalism by the late John Tyndall.

One of the functions of the A.K. Chesterton Trust is to preserve and keep in print important works on British Nationalism. This particular book has been rare for many years.

We hope that this new edition will enable a new generation of British Nationalists to study and learn from this formative work.


**Colin Todd**

The A.K. Chesterton Trust
October 2012

# FOREWORD

## by John Tyndall

The British nation has a heritage of human skills and qualities second to none in the world. Its peoples and their offspring have colonised, and still rule, enormous areas of the earth, containing immense natural wealth. The British have not known defeat in war for two hundred years.

Yet today Britain is rapidly being left behind. She cannot modernise her industries and services. She cannot decently house her population. She cannot make use of her best brains. She cannot pay her way among the nations. She cannot defend her interests throughout the world. She cannot stem her mounting wave of crime and anarchy. While nations defeated by Britain in battle grow strong and prosperous, Britain herself muddles on from crisis to crisis, while millions of her people still live in surroundings of squalor, ugliness and wretchedness in cities that became out of date at the end of the last century.

What is the cause of this condition? Why does this most gifted nation fail to hold its own today? Why has Britain won the war, but not succeeded in winning the peace?

The truth is that for the past half-century British genius and British strength have been paralysed by a poverty of leadership, by archaic political institutions and by naive and flabby political philosophies; by a system that has given the greatest power to the smallest men and which has divided the nation against itself in an endless clash of party rivalries and sectional conflicts.

Most of all, the weakness of Britain today is the product of an intelligentsia which during living memory has been hypnotised by the madness of liberalism and internationalism, before which altars an unending succession of British interests have been sacrificed — to the impoverishment of British power and to the profit of Britain's enemies, not all of whom lie East of the Iron Curtain.

For these follies we now approach greater crisis than ever before — not merely the transient crisis out of which one party can gain advantage by blaming another, but a deeper crisis of national existence which is the product of many decades of slow rot in the body politic.

While crisis dawns, the older political parties of the day can do no better than to fight sham battles over the trivia of daily life, lowering the tone of British politics to new depths but utterly impervious to the central fact of national catastrophe.

What can be done? Where lies our way out of the present muddle? This booklet proposes an answer through principles of firm action embodied in a dynamic new political faith. It is the faith of British Nationalism — as seen through the eyes of one of Britain's post-war generation who have revolted against the spirit of national surrender endemic in current times, and who represent a new force in political life to which Britain is paying growing attention.

This is not an election manifesto; not a set of slogans devised to goad unthinking folk for the purpose of cheap votes. Its aim is to help in rallying serious people to great long-term national tasks. It therefore proclaims broad principles of faith rather than attempt a solution to every minute issue of the moment. British Nationalism will not win through quickly or easily. We must expect long struggle before its influence becomes decisive on the political stage. For the purpose of this struggle it is important that Nationalists are united on firm essentials, even if they may differ over small details. This brief work aims to arrange and clarify such essentials in a form understandable to those new to the Nationalist movement and its ideas. What is written represents an individual view and does not imply the complete endorsement of any political party except where stated by such. It represents, in main essence, the aspirations of the British Nationalist movement generally, and is a guide to all who seek to know the nature of this movement and its aims.

# 1. NATIONALISM- POLICY AND FAITH

Throughout our lifetime the internationalist illusion has gripped the minds of the politicians of Britain. Cutting across all party differences has been their faith in the international organisation of the world and their belief in the common aims of mankind. All British policy, political, economic and military, has been subordinated to this belief. Vital British assets and interests have been sacrificed to the international cause. British sovereignty and freedom have been placed in jeopardy. Dependence has been preferred to independence. Idle dreams of an international Utopia have been made a substitute for national self reliance and national strength.

The utopia has not come. Mankind is, as ever, divided by conflicts of nationality, race, ideology and economic interest. Meanwhile Britain has been dangerously weakened in her capacity to survive in a competitive world. We have paid a bitter price for our escape into fairyland.

It is against this background that the new and growing Nationalist movement in this country has been born.

We hear Nationalist slogans and sentiments uttered all over the world, but not so often here in Britain. What is British Nationalism?

It should be defined first of all as the creed of faith in ourselves: faith in our qualities and traditions; faith in our capacity to build our own future in our own way and by our own hands; faith in our great destiny as a nation.

We Nationalists believe wholeheartedly in the assertion of the independence and sovereignty of Britain in world affairs and in the affirmation of her place as a great power in her own right. We completely oppose the subordination of British policy to that of the United States or UNO, and we reject as dangerous the growing campaign to place the resources of the nations under a centralised international control.

We believe that the future of the British people rests, not on treaties, summit conferences and international goodwill, but on our own strength and resourcefulness as a nation, our own determination, our own effort and our own self-confidence.

Today we are continually being told that the world has grown smaller and that nations must be 'interdependent' with one another. In the case of some nations this is undoubtedly true. What is also true is that only those nations who have the means and the courage to remain self-dependent can qualify for the description of great and free. We believe it is right for Britain to be great and remain free.

This does not mean that we stand for the cutting off of Britain from the rest of the world and the rejection of all forms of collaboration between the nations. But we hold that Britain should contribute to these things as a strong and free national entity, not, as at present, as a second class colony of the Dollar Empire. Cooperation we support; interdependence we oppose.

The very word 'interdependence' is in any event misleading in the context of today. It provides merely a softening phrase under which the weaker powers of the world are swallowed into the orbit of the stronger ones. Everyone knows what is meant today when the politicians speak of our 'interdependence' with America: it means their cowardly desertion of Britain's position in the world and their lame surrender to dollar hegemony. Under the guise of this term our national economy, our foreign policy and our means of self-defence have to all practical purposes been taken out of British hands. 'Interdependence' thoroughly suits the powers anxious to tighten their control over the nations. It is a much milder term than conquest.

Interdependence is variously justified as a virtue and as a necessity. To few except an incurable minority of one-world leftists is it a virtue. Is it, from our point of view, a necessity?

Certainly the post-war era has seen a decline in British power at the same time as it has seen the rise of vast new powers. But has this been inevitable or has it been willed by our political leaders? The so-called 'inevitability' of Britain's shrinking power status would seem a strange doctrine indeed to anyone looking at a map of the British Empire and Commonwealth that survived the last two wars entirely intact. For reasons justifiable only in their own distorted imaginations, the leaders of this Empire and Commonwealth have spent the last two or three decades allowing it to disintegrate. No great armed foe has invaded it and taken it away by force. It has just been allowed to fall apart.

Meanwhile the moulders of political opinion have hammered into an almost sacred article of faith the idea that this disintegration has been a just and necessary process. Millions have believed them without ever really thinking why.

The other great empires of the world have not in the meantime been afflicted with this masochistic urge to become weaker and smaller, but have single-mindedly expanded in size and strength. That the present balance of power weighs so heavily in their favour and against Britain is not the verdict of almighty providence but only of differing attitudes of national leadership and will; of the will to live as distinct from the will to die. We are where we are today because our leaders have been dominated by the will to die.

Nations in this state of mind will always cling to straws of salvation such as 'interdependence' and 'collective security', so beloved by the liberal theorists because they provide a substitute for national fibre and an excuse for national weakness. What is easier and more comfortable when our British problems become too much for our politicians to cope with than for those politicians to seek cause and solution in the climate of international relationships rather than the substance of Britain itself and in their own capacity, or lack of it, to mould that substance to our advantage! Behind the sweet phrases that announce the internationalist dream lies the tragic sense of national impotence. The phrases are the thoughts of the tired and the doubting who have lost faith in Britain; who have lost faith in themselves as Britons.

We Nationalists have neither lost faith in Britain nor the British race. We believe that there is no fundamental weakness in our nation that cannot be cured through the emergence of new leadership. It is our intention eventually to provide that leadership and to provide the policies by which Britain can climb back to her former position and regain her confidence and self-respect. This is the meaning of the Nationalist movement.

In another most important respect a more national approach to our affairs is needed. For too long we have been ruled by people who imagine that they derive their mandate from the world at large and that in consequence they have an obligation to the world at large that must on occasions override their obligations to their own country and its citizens. This outlook results in a quite absurd allocation of British energies and resources to the solving of other nations problems, in many cases problems that happen to be utterly insoluble except on the initiative and through the action of those nations concerned themselves. For the private philanthropist to take upon himself the burdens of mankind in general rather than those near to him and within his capacity to bear is to many people an odd choice of priorities, but at least he has the right to make such a choice — it is his money. But when politicians appoint themselves as philanthropists to the universe in preference to devoting every available resource to national needs — and in doing so make use of other people's (i.e the taxpayers) money then it becomes more than just odd; it becomes criminal.

To the Nationalist it is inconceivable that the resources of one's country and the energies of one's countrymen should be directed to any purpose but the welfare of those at home and the prosperity and development of the nation to which all belong — for at least as long as there are any shortcomings in those departments. And shortcomings there assuredly are, and for a long time will be, in the welfare of British people and the prosperity and development of Britain.

We see in these related examples the two twin insanities of the internationalist mind. Firstly, the assumption that we can rely upon the preparedness of the rest of the world to help us: secondly, the assumption that it is our duty to help the rest of the world. While these sentiments might be perfectly laudable and workable within a single society and between related people, they just do not operate within the world as a whole. In any event, even between individuals the principle of good neighbourliness, fine though it is, is not allowed by the self-respecting person to become the prerequisite for existence. Self-respecting and sensible nations, likewise, liaise and cooperate where mutual advantage indicates, but only pauper nations lean on others for life and only monumentally stupid nations subsidise others for life.

Nationalism has one final and vital role: it must restore unity to the British people. Today we are torn apart by all manner of factional interests representing class, occupation, religion and political ideology. Three major parties argue with one another over details of day to day government which are superfluous as long as they exist within the overall framework of a weak and lethargic national body. Sections of industry, goaded from the rear by political exploiters, fight over the spoils of the nation's production. Social groupings, representing manual workers and brain workers, are encouraged to identify themselves with conflicting political causes and to believe that the interests of one must always be pursued to the detriment of the interests of the other and that the state of the country is the fault of the other.

Only a community of people with a truly national sense will be immune to the insidious disease of class warfare. For brief periods in two world wars the British community captured this ability to think in national terms, and worked together in a way in which it has never done since. This national sense must be restored. But it cannot be restored by politicians preoccupied with the hoary conflicts of years past in which one section of society was perpetually divided from another, nor by men who offer to our people no more than a dull and humble position in the world and whose every utterance echoes the tune of national defeatism and twilight. The triumph of Nationalism in Britain will only come from the leadership of men who are identified heart and soul with the cause of Britain, who recognise no other cause or loyalty than to the people of Britain and who have faith in the capacity of the British nation to accomplish any task and meet any challenge with which life may confront it.

# 2. BRITAIN AS A WORLD POWER

By far the most significant development of the 20th Century has been the rise to dominance of the new continental-scale monster states, creating entirely new dimensions of political, economic and military power.

It has been said often enough, and with truth, that mere size does not bestow upon a state the quality of greatness. National character, technical skill and efficient organisation are more important. But given these things there is no doubt today that a nation's strength and security are that much greater and its future that much more assured for its being very large, rather than middle-sized or small. Modern facilities of communication have made space an asset rather than a hindrance; modem technology has set a premium on the world's great reservoirs of raw material; modern mass production has underlined the importance of the great internal market.

By virtue of these conditions the United States and Russia have emerged as the dominant powers of today and the apparent arbiters of the future. In the face of this build up of power the governing doctrine of Britain in the post-war world has been one of resignation to a diminishing status and subservient position in relation to the new giants, and by virtue of this a policy of helpless commitment to the former. This policy has been raised to the level of almost unquestioned dogma, branding as wild heresy any concept of a British future except under American patronage and protection and in step with American designs.

Yet a moment's thought will expose the falsehood of this doctrine.

The balance of power in the world as we see it today is not something that has descended upon us from heaven; it is the product of recent history, of what men have done or failed to do during the last century or so.

The same thrust of expansion that created the American and Russian power systems as we now know them also created a whole British world of infinite wealth and opportunity: a world in which our people could live in prosperity, strength and freedom for unlimited centuries to come. In the boundless lands of Empire and Commonwealth lie all the ingredients of modern power, wanting only for a determined national policy aiming at their full coordination and development in the service of the British future. Failure to produce such a policy has been the overriding weakness of British statecraft over the past century. Failure to exploit, or even understand, our paramount national asset has frustrated the building of Greater Britain and produced the modern abortion of mini-Britain.

There is yet time, although not much time, to redeem this failure.

We must not only recognise the Commonwealth as the singular source of our future existence; we must urgently begin to remake the Commonwealth into a genuine instrument of national power.

The first step in this direction is to create for the Commonwealth a real mechanism of political and economic unity.

This itself is a task which calls for the highest statesmanship, since it must treat our older Dominions — the hard core of the Commonwealth — not as subordinate colonies but as free and equal partners, with firmly established traditions of sovereignty in the handling of their own affairs. The eventual aim should be a central coordinating body chosen from the main Commonwealth lands. This could be operative on a mobile basis sitting alternately in the various countries represented, or it could function from a newly appointed Commonwealth federal capital, preferably situated outside Britain. Whilst in former times it would have been impossible to reconcile such a system with efficiency and quickness of decision, today everything is feasible on account of the amazing development of intercontinental transport and telecommunication by satellite.

Our ruling Commonwealth council should be responsible for the formulation of policy in major fields such as foreign relations, economic development, trade, defence, scientific and industrial research and migration. Its powers of execution would obviously be limited by the right of self-governing members to accept or reject its policies. However, in practice there is little doubt that the obvious benefits to each in prosperity and security would lead to acceptance in all reasonable cases. The British nations today have the option of mutually coordinating their affairs by some common control or of subordinating those affairs to an unwelcome foreign control. This fact should not be hard to make understood by all concerned.

What countries should be members of this association? The obvious candidates are the United Kingdom, Canada, Australia, New Zealand, South Africa and Rhodesia. In all of these countries except one, people of British stock are in control and in most cases form the bulk of the population. With South Africa we have common interests in trade and defence which can be made to transcend the old Boer War rivalries and the not so old bitterness that has arisen from contemporary British anti-white policy. But reconciliation with South Africa and British Rhodesia will only be possible on the basis of our acceptance of those countries internal policies. We should do more than acknowledge acceptance; we should give complete support.

Other countries — and we are speaking now of the Coloured Commonwealth — who wish to benefit from an association with us and who can offer us some benefit in return may be considered for membership, but on the terms laid down by the senior members. There can be no question of South Africa or Rhodesia, or for that matter Britain, adjusting racial policies to suit them. Nor can there be any question of the senior Commonwealth members being obliged to subsidise inefficient economies without having any control over those economies. Coloured states that demand recognition of their freedom must be free in effect as well as in name.

If we consider only the six mentioned countries, this Commonwealth would represent a world power of combined area as great as Russia, with a European population of nearly a hundred millions, of which about 85 to 90 percent would be of British stock. The area would represent a super-abundance of natural wealth of almost every kind, with a vast fund of human skills ready to find substitutes for any materials that were in short supply. Such an area could, and should, become economically self supporting and militarily strong enough to deter aggression by any other power unaided. This would provide the basis for an entirely free role in world affairs, unfettered by the dictates of UNO or any other international grouping. We would have the means, provided we had the will, to pursue an entirely independent British destiny, friendly to other powers but in no way reliant upon them.

By a coordination of the best scientific brains and resources of the whole Commonwealth we could afford to explore new technological fields far beyond those open to us today with the limited means imposed by our division. We could equal, and perhaps surpass, America as the world's most advanced technological power — particularly as we could create opportunities that would lure back to the Commonwealth those many fine technicians that we have currently lost through the brain drain.

Within the Commonwealth we should pursue a massive programme of migration under which millions would be resettled from crowded Britain into the great spaces of the Dominions, thus establishing better and healthier living conditions, free from congestion and excessive urbanism and lessening the strategic danger of being too concentrated. At the same time we should develop increasingly cheaper means of communication so as to enable much closer contact between the widespread communities.

Through a coordinated educational programme we should seek to encourage in all our new generations a common patriotism that would overcome the great distances that separate the different parts of the British race, and thereby facilitate the operation of a common policy for the whole.

It may be asked, how can there be any certainty that the countries concerned will be prepared to comply with such a scheme? The answer is that it is the job of statecraft, not to predict certainties, but to point to desirable and necessary objectives. No great objective in the building of Britain was undertaken with the certainty that it would be achieved, only with the will to achieve it and the knowledge that it had to be achieved. However, the politicians of our times are planning world systems much more fantastic in their assumptions and much more unnatural in their structure. The very people who question whether our system is possible seem not to question the possibility of these other schemes.

The creation of a unified British world system is an enormously difficult task today, but it is possible with the right leadership and will. And if it can be created it has a much greater possibility of surviving than the synthetic internationalist world orders being proposed by our opponents.

By the combination of the attributes of close on 100 millions of the world's most dynamic and creative people, and the immense fund of natural riches that would be at their command, we have in this prospect the makings of a civilisation that could surpass in its splendour anything yet achieved in the history of man — if only our people can be awakened to the greatness of such a task in time.

But before anything can be done we must put an end to the present indecisive balancing act by which we run around trying to maintain the Commonwealth (in the most unworkable and unprofitable form) while talking about a 'special relationship' with America and flirting with European union. We cannot have it all three ways. We can become part of the American or European systems and say goodbye to any kind of future as a free nation, or we can build a Commonwealth system based on solid foundations of British kinship which can guarantee a great British future for ages to come. We cannot pursue all at the same time.

We Nationalists choose the path of free development within the Commonwealth because it is the only path compatible with the retention of our nationhood, and indeed the only path that will secure a system that will work by virtue of being held together by really enduring bonds.

This great objective must not be beyond the strength of our generation.

# 3. ECONOMIC NATIONALISM

The term 'national economy' is one that we hear regularly in day to day jargon. In fact it is a misnomer. Britain's economy, as presently constituted, is not national but international. Its stability and strength are constantly affected by the ups and downs of international trade. Its growth rests on the international market. Its whole direction and planning are subject to international conditions.

Britain, most of all the world's powers, is not master of her economic policies.

As long as the British economic machine is organised to depend for so much of its business on international trade this position will continue. Britain can hope to have no economic future except by permission of its foreign customers and suppliers.

Everyone knows how this has come about. Britain pioneered the Industrial Revolution and was the first modem industrial power. The whole world then wanted her manufactured goods and the industries that supplied them expanded to cater for a market far in excess of that which could be found at home in the British Isles. At the same time these goods had to be paid for and Britain agreed to import huge quantities of food and other primary products to balance the trade. British output of these products contracted to make way for those from abroad. Our farming industry shrank, the land was deserted and the crowded urban slum became the dwelling place of millions of our countrymen and women. In this way we created the unbalanced, specialised economy under which we have lived since.

Inevitably, our world domination of the industrial market has faded away as other powers have learnt our techniques and followed us into the field, creating intensive competition sometimes aided by cheaper prices, derived from sweated labour, which we could not hope to match except by paying our own workers atrocious wages. We tried to do this for a time, and hence the appalling conditions that characterised many of our industrial towns and gave rise to Twentieth Century Socialism. Socialism, however, failed to get to the root of the trouble — which was Britain's commitment to an international cut-price system. While an enormous proportion of Britain's produce had to compete on world markets with that of countries which paid starvation wages the British worker would forever be denied a fair remuneration for his efforts.

The system has been with us to this day. Now we are just another industrial nation, with a manufactured surplus which we must somehow keep unloading in a market where foreign producers are all trying to do exactly the same thing and where supply is certain to eventually out-pace demand; also a market which can at times fluctuate crazily through bouts of speculation and political instability.

It needs no great economic insight to see that where Britain is concerned such a system must lead inevitably to collapse. The danger signals of this collapse appeared during the Thirties, when British industry almost ground to a halt and millions trudged the streets looking for work. It was postponed by the war, which first absorbed labour into the forces and armaments industries and later put some of Britain's main competitors out of the field while their damaged factories had to be rebuilt. Now, with these competitors recovered, all the old symptoms of collapse are reappearing and the desperate measures employed by recent governments to bolster up trade abroad — particularly Harold Wilson's policy of devaluation — represent nothing more than cardboard barriers erected to stem a tidal flood.

Many extra factors have intervened in Britain's case to worsen the position still more: chronic laziness, inefficiency and an antiquated industrial relations structure have made us even less fit to maintain our place in the world trade jungle than we would normally have been. These abuses must be drastically remedied, but even when they are and industry is raised to the maximum pitch of modern capacity, it would only delay the collapse; it would not stop it.

For just as simple mathematical law rules that you cannot pour a quart of water into a pint pot without half of it splashing over the edges and onto the ground, by the same law it is clear that an economy organised to cater for a market in which it cannot sell what it can produce must run down and eventually go broke!

This, put in the most basic of terms, is the process that the British economy is following today.

Essentially, the problem facing all the productive forces of Britain is that of finding a market which can be relied upon to expand and consume their goods at a rate commensurate with that at which they can be produced when industry is fully harnessed to the powers of modem science. Or put more simply: how can we make it commercially possible to sell what it is technically and humanly possible to produce?

This was no problem to Britain in the early days of industrial supremacy; it is the crucial problem now. But in fact we are still organised as if these early days remained with us. Our Twentieth Century economy is geared to Nineteenth Century conditions!

It is the nations that are geared to the conditions of today that will inevitably control the world. It is the nations that can find markets for the full volume of modern production that will be the powers of the coming era. This fact transcends all current arguments about Capitalism and Socialism. Industry, whether run under private or state ownership, is faced with the same laws of existence. For every producer there must be a buyer. Goods, as long as they rot in warehouses, are valueless. Machines justify their existence, not from the volume of goods that they can produce, but from the proportion of those goods that can be sold.

Finding the market to absorb wealth produced — not disputes over its ownership — is the vital issue of economic policy.

America has always been in a position to contend with the machine age better than we have in Britain. The reason is elementary. America has the world's largest home market in terms of purchasing power. This market can absorb everything, or very nearly everything, that American machinery can produce. The American economy has grown to a structure aimed primarily to cater for this home market, with foreign trade merely spice on the cake, as it were. The latter represents less than 10 per-cent of America's total business, while it represents more than 30 per-cent of the business of our own country. Whatever the uncertainty of foreign markets, American producers have such immense purchasing power at home that they have a head start on anyone else in the struggle for industrial expansion.

Britain does not have this purchasing power at home and quite clearly the rest of the world is not going to stand still and halt its own industrial development in order to keep markets open for British producers to sell in as if by divine right. We will not, as long as our eyes are fixed on international horizons, discover new buyers in quantities that will replace the old or in quantities that will keep pace with the ever increasing power of industry to make goods. Our only hope for the future is to find a very large and growing market which we can control and organise ourselves, combatting foreign competition by protective tariffs and mobilising our productive forces to cater for this market in full. By being organised in this way America and Russia have become the world's foremost industrial powers. We must organise in the same way to survive alongside them.

For the British economy to develop in such a way we need a vast economic area capable of supporting an expanding population as a continually increasing fund of home purchasing power and practically self-supporting in the raw materials needed to sustain modem industry under present conditions.

Today some unthinking people are suggesting European Union as an answer to this need. It is no answer. A great part of the European economy is based on the same predominance of manufacturing as is that of Britain. Europe, like Britain, has a shortage of space and raw materials. It only recreates the problem of our island economy on a larger scale. Furthermore, and most important of all, its peoples are not united by kinship and cannot be kept together by any bond other than mutual economic interest — which is the very last bond that they in fact have. The politicians who hope that by scuttling into Europe they will create an economic United States are sadly out of touch with the realities of modern economic power and of the human factors that play a part in it.

Britain, however, has an alternative to the small island economy of the present and to the flimsy trading alliance of Europe. She can exploit, as she has never yet seriously tried to do. The mighty potential of a united Commonwealth — of Greater Britain.

Within such a Commonwealth, bound together by the ethnic unity of the peoples of British stock, there exist all the prerequisites for an economy of American-type dimensions: abundant space for the rearing of a huge population without unhealthy overcrowding, creating the same kind of purchasing potential that has enabled America to exploit mass production to the full; at the same time almost every raw material in super abundance to supply the wheels of industry without recourse to international exchange except among kindred peoples operating through a central coordinating machinery.

In this way all the dangers and insecurities of the present anarchic world system could be avoided. Industry could produce for an assured market the expansion of which could be guaranteed. Primary products would be in assured supply. The planning so much desired by Socialists would be possible by way of being freed from the unplanned impact of foreign crises and depressions. The enterprise that is the cornerstone of the Conservative faith would be fair enterprise, not subjected to the hindrance of cut-price foreign competition. The best features of both doctrines could be made to work by their synthesis in a higher doctrine: economic nationalism; the organisation of the production and distribution of wealth within the secure framework of a mighty nation-state.

In the same way as Commonwealth Government should supervise trade between its parts so should it supervise the all important forces of finance. Today International Finance rules our lives, with its supra-national loyalties and objectives. It transfers its activities crazily from one part of the world to another according to where capital can be deployed for the greatest profit. Based in one country, it may finance the industries of another to compete with those on its doorstep which are crying out for investment. By controlling the means of productive and purchasing power it can ruin, not only whole industries, but whole nations which fail to comply with its own policies of self-interest.

In recent years in particular the forces of International Finance have become dangerously involved in political developments which are clearly subversive to the interests of the Western nations — the uprooting of Belgian power in the Congo, the world sanctions campaign against Rhodesia and the financing of student revolution everywhere being prominent examples. Many people are coming to believe that International Finance has a vested interest in the creeping internationalisation of the world, and that behind all the slogans about 'peace' and 'brotherhood' lurk sinister designs which are likely to place total world control in the hands of a few ruthless financial operators.

The British nation must be freed from the clutches of the international financial system and must firmly control all the financial forces by which its economy is fed. This means strong government direction of financial enterprise within defined national and Commonwealth bounds, and based on a regular equilibrium between the creation of money and the real wealth in production.

All this should not be taken to infer that either Britain or the Commonwealth should withdraw from international trade. To suggest that would be ludicrous. But a national system such as that proposed here would mean that our reliance on international trade would be greatly less than at the present time, and that we would therefore be equipped at all times to adopt extra national measures in any world emergency. At the same time by basing our productive machinery on a vast and wealthy home market we would, like America, be able to be much more competitive internationally. World trade should represent, as has been said before, the spice on the cake — not the bread and butter.

Again the objection to a Commonwealth system will be raised on the grounds of feasibility. It will be claimed that Commonwealth countries have evolved too far away from Britain and towards

American and Asian trade contacts to readily come into line with such an arrangement. However, we must remember that it is precisely the lack of a proper Commonwealth policy here in Britain that has caused our old partners to travel in this direction. We are not right now trying to get into Europe because we have lost the support of the Commonwealth; we have been losing the support of the Commonwealth because, among other reasons, we have been turning to Europe. Present attitudes of pessimism with regard to Britain's influence with the Commonwealth commit the fault of confusing cause with effect. If our influence has declined it has been because of our policies at home, not because of the desires of the Commonwealth.

The task of persuading Commonwealth countries to adopt our system will not be an easy and straightforward one such as it would have been several decades ago. But, as was pointed out in the last chapter, much wilder and less feasible schemes have become the governing policies of our current leaders, whether Labour or Conservative. World systems, alliances, trading areas and mutual security blocs are espoused, plotted and blueprinted which have none of the unifying elements such as are needed to make them work, whether the elements of complementary economic structures, common political interests or plain and simple kinship. In this concept of the Commonwealth — which, as has already been explained, consists mainly of the White Commonwealth — the basic unifying elements do exist, even if changes have to be made from the policies and trends of the last 20 years. Of all the alternatives facing us this is the most feasible.

Within a national system utilising to the full all the immense resources that our Commonwealth has to offer in both natural wealth and human skill we can develop a new economic strength of such magnitude as to not only secure our future prosperity and standard of life but furthermore bring about a complete revolution in the existing balances of world power — confronting the Communist and American blocs with a new giant of not so far off their proportions and with much greater homogeneity. It could mean a British future brighter and more fruitful than even the greatest periods of the British past.

This is the meaning of the choice between national organisation and international chaos.

# 4. PRESERVING THE BRITISH

All that has been said so far about British Nationalism and Greater Britain must be conditional upon the survival of the British as a people: of the distinct qualities inherited from past generations who raised Britain to supremacy. Factors of leadership and political and economic organisation which influence our position today — these can be changed. But if ever the basic character of the British people were to alter and their inherent qualities be lost, then no amount of improvement in their institutions would avail against the certainty of a dark future.

This is the fact that looms behind the much discussed race issue. Behind all the conflicts and hatreds that fester on the surface of present race relations lies the fundamental wish, need and right of our people to maintain their historical identity and the traditional living habits and customs to which they are attached. These are quite clearly endangered by current attempts at racial integration being made by the authorities in Britain, with the aid both of indoctrination and police coercion.

If other nations can ignore the race issue — except just to comment on it sanctimoniously from the lofty heights of isolation — certainly we in Britain cannot. It affects us at home in the form of a growing immigrant population; it affects us overseas, where our kinsfolk live as minorities in mainly coloured lands. All over the world racial unrest smoulders behind the frontage of international disputes. The race problem bids with certainty to be one of the two or three dominating issues of the remainder of this century.

With the coming to the forefront of this stormy question we have witnessed the rise of a new self-appointed priesthood, tramping the continents and haranguing the peoples with idealistic solutions based neither on the facts of history or science nor on any real regard for human nature, only on an emotional jargon bolstered up by a self-debasing pseudo-morality.

Today this priesthood, which numbers among its adherents many of our so-called 'intelligentsia', has a new bogey word with which it seeks to evoke popular guilt and hysteria. The word is 'Powellism', and it is flung as if it were the curse of Satan at every person or organisation which dares to question the wisdom of importing a large racial problem into our country and of seeking to overcome this problem by enforced integration.

What is called 'Powellism' in fact reflects the deepest and most instinctive revulsion of the vast mass of the British people against what it knows to be the imposition of something utterly alien upon our land and our society. It is a revulsion felt, if not often loudly expressed, by all but a small minority of poisoned minds and atrophied souls who happen to prevail strongly in the opinion-forming media and in the corridors of political power—in short, the priesthood.

'Powellism' is in any event an inaccurate term. Mr Enoch Powell has only articulated and given new voice to a sentiment which persisted for many years and on an issue on which others warned for many years before he spoke his first words about it in 1968. He should be complimented and supported for what he has said and he should be encouraged to say more, but it is ludicrous to attribute to him a race awareness and race feeling that preceded his speeches on the subject by probably two decades.

On race the morality of the priesthood has a simple answer to everything. All men are equal; race means nothing except for the colour of the skin; the races must mix and become one, and all who object to that are either deficient in education or mentally ill; the lower position of the coloured man is due entirely to his brutal treatment by the whites not on any account to his own deficiencies; black is always right and white is always wrong; when whites riot against blacks they are bigoted fascist thugs persecuting the helpless, but when blacks riot against whites they are brave and noble idealists campaigning for their rights and in no way to blame for the bloodshed involved. Under the auspices of this new priesthood the white world becomes spellbound by self-guilt, unable even to discuss the racial problem in a reasoned and practical way, and prepared to sanction what must end in the sacrifice of its own existence for the sake of repentance.

Is all this frenzy helping the coloured man?

In fact the more intensive the effort to integrate coloured and white societies the more aggravated does racial tension become. In our own country this can be seen as clearly as anywhere. A few years ago racial ill feeling was almost unknown amongst us. The few coloureds that were here were reacted to with friendly interest and sympathy. Now everything has changed. The mass influx of Africans and West Indians, Indians and Pakistanis, and the fanatical campaign to push them into white homes, hotels, boarding houses, clubs, factories and offices has resulted in a massive and seething hatred, with people who a few years ago had no racial feelings whatsoever now harbouring bitter antagonism towards all coloureds as a result of their personal experiences. Inevitably, the coloured man is the first to suffer.

Exactly the same position has been created m the United States under the sponsorship of 'Civil Rights'.

On the other hand, what has happened when the coloured peoples have been given power in lands formerly ruled by colonists? In almost every case the fruits of power have gone to just a privileged few, i.e. the coloured dictators and their small circles of flatterers, while the ordinary masses suffer a poverty and a tyranny many times worse than any known under their old masters. Bankruptcy is rife, starvation and rioting the rule and imprisonment without trial the customary reward for anyone who objects.

No-one who seriously and sincerely wants to help the coloured man towards a better deal can believe that this is the way. Only those who in their odious hypocrisy wish to use the coloureds as a weapon for their own political ends can do so.

We believe the way of Nationalism is a better way.

We are British Nationalists first and foremost and are determined to preserve our British civilisation in the many areas of the world where it has taken root. We don't want to change this civilisation and live under another one. We don't want to change our national character and assume a new and different national character; we want to stay as we are giving to the world those particular things which our inborn qualities as a people have fitted us to give. We may be terribly 'unprogressive' in this attitude, but this is how we feel and we know that the British people in the majority are behind us.

We know that racial integration along the lines now being pursued by marxists, liberals and one-worlders is bound to lead to the loss of our identity as a people and of that particular genius that has been Britain's gift to history.

It is no refutation of this to trot out the old tale about the British being a mixed stock. Our only mixture is of stocks of North Western Europe closely akin to each other and blended together like the branches of a family tree. This is something entirely different from interbreeding with races of completely alien background and character, such as those indigenous to Africa and Asia.

We therefore oppose racial integration and stand for racial separateness, that is the separate development of the different races and nations along lines corresponding to their differing qualities.

This means the safeguarding of our own identity as Britons, but it means more than that; it means a genuine attempt at harmony between the races along realistic lines by the encouragement of the coloured peoples towards a similar sense of identity and towards a development suited to their own particular characteristics.

This has for years been the policy adopted in Southern Africa. It is a policy which has worked for the betterment of both white and black, as can be seen by a comparison of the living standards of the latter with those of their fellow Africans to the North. Such a policy should command our wholehearted support.

Its implementation where Britain is concerned means two things: firstly that we call a halt to all further immigration of coloured races into our own homeland — yes, including those who get in under the guise of being so-called 'dependents' — and that we work towards the gradual and humane resettlement of our existing coloured population in the lands of their origin. In this latter connection we must be careful to steer clear of misleading concepts such as 'voluntary repatriation'. If left to themselves, our immigrants are not going to all go home; the great majority of them will stay here, where they can enjoy vastly higher standards than they were used to before they came. To talk of voluntary repatriation amounts to no more than cowardly compromise with fashionable 'liberal' trends of opinion and talk which when seriously examined in this context amount to pure imbecility. To make a scheme of repatriation really work in the long term interests of white and coloured races we must have the courage to make it obligatory and furthermore to have the courage to say so honestly and openly and not try to mislead the public of this country.

Secondly, we must put an end to the insanity of sabotaging the colonial achievements of our own kinfolk elsewhere in the Commonwealth and we must support them in their efforts to maintain order and progress for all races within a system based on an understanding of the diverse attributes and needs of each.

**Britons have not sailed the oceans and built new British civilisations out of jungle and wilderness merely for our generation to pull them down. They have not stayed loyal to us in two world wars merely for us to turn now and stab them in the back.**

This rule is applicable to all areas of the earth where British wealth has been created by British brains and leadership. It is applicable today particularly to Rhodesia, where a brave handful of our people fight to preserve a part of the British heritage against the organised venom of the world's liberals and leftists. Britons here at home should realise that the white settlers fighting to retain their position are fighting for our cause and for our future, the future of British civilisation the world over.

The Rhodesian issue is, make no mistake, a racial issue. On its solution depends the question of whether the magnificent achievements of that small country remain in the hands of those who created them and thereby serve to enrich the British future or whether they pass into irresponsible hands and waste away into uselessness and decay. We have seen the danger signal in what has happened elsewhere in Africa. Let us take heed of it.

And over the Rhodesian issue let us in particular guard against those deceivers in the ranks of 'Conservatism' who pose as friends of our kinfolk in Rhodesia and talk of the need to build bridges to them while at the same time kow-towing to the leftist principle of 'eventual majority rule'. When the doctrines of these swindlers are put under the microscope they become exposed as no better than those of the liberals, communists and open enemies of the whites in Africa. They merely propose to put off till tomorrow what the latter intend to do today. White Rhodesians and South Africans should be under no illusions; they should recognise that their only true friends in this country are those who are prepared to speak out openly in defence of their right to stay in power for all time and not just for the few more years of grace that our modern Tories would condescend to give them.

Once we recognise the underlying facts of race which have affected the whole development of Africa and Asia, and which so much affect the future existence of Britain itself, we can, as the Rhodesians and South Africans are doing, extend our consideration to the coloured peoples and help them to find a role in which they can advance in a way most conducive to their own security and happiness. The way to do this is to provide them with work suited to their own capacities and with progressively better rates of pay, decent houses in their own townships where they may mingle harmoniously with their own kind, social services that care for their health and general well being and opportunity to express themselves through their own tribal traditions and customs. All these things are now being put into practice in Southern Africa in a way that does far more service to the cause of the Negro than all the egalitarian rantings of the Huddlestons, the Brockways and the Peter Hains.

The essential difference between this practical policy and the woolly dreams of the liberals and multi-racialists is that it is based on the simple principle of white leadership. We, like the leaders of South Africa and Rhodesia, accept without guilt or shame the truth upon which this principle is based and which the overwhelming weight of history supports: **that while every race may have its particular skills and qualities the capacity to govern and lead and sustain civilisation as we understand it lies essentially with the European**. To give the coloured man a better life is a worthy aim — providing one is sincere about it and not just trying to pose as an obedient disciple of 'approved opinion'. But to give him power and responsibility which he is ill fitted to use wisely is something entirely different, and in fact ends by defeating his quest for a better life.

It is right that we should continue to help the coloured man—not as an act of patronage or charity, which does no service to his self-respect, but in return for his helping us. But we do not intend to blow up in flames the fruits of two to three hundred years of our ancestors endeavour merely in order to appease the amateur fads of one misguided decade.

We have spoken of helping other races. But let us not be hypocrites: while we want to do this, our first duty and concern is our own race: the protection of its interests, the advancement of its power. By a manly determination to do this we can best come to an understanding with the African and Asian who care for their interests. Such people, in their simplicity, hate cant and despise self-flagellation. By grovelling to them on our hands and knees, as successive British governments of recent times have made a habit of doing, we only invite contempt — which does nothing at all to help harmony.

Mutual respect, based on this rule, is the only way to settle this most explosive of questions.

# 5. DUTIES OF GOVERNMENT

Strong, wise and honest government is desperately needed in Britain today — more than at any time before. Yet now is the time when weak and dishonest government is most in evidence. Let us face the issue: our modern democracy has got out of hand. It neither governs responsibly nor is in fact democracy. It combines the worst of two polar opposites: it is anarchy at one end of the scale and dictatorship at the other. It is anarchical in its failure to exercise true leadership and authority in the great national tasks where leadership and authority are most needed; it is dictatorial in its pursuit of policies for which it has no mandate from the electorate. It represents the art of government brought to its very lowest level, where bribery, flattery and deceit are the essentials of success and where the national weal becomes subordinated in an orgy of factional conflicts and personal drives for power. At various times in the history of every nation affairs have reached this state, where the sediment has risen to the top, the political tradition has been perverted and corruption rules the scene. At such times bold surgery has had to be applied or else the social order has collapsed and the national body decayed into oblivion. Britain has reached such a state now. We are in a crisis that is at root a crisis of leadership.

Never before in British life have the standards of leadership, integrity and public duty been as low as now. Never has so ludicrous a selection of ruling figures occupied the national stage. Never have government policies been so clearly shaped by the rat-race for cheap electoral advantage and in desertion of the real needs of the nation. Government and politicians in Britain today have, hardly surprisingly, earned the deepest contempt of all but the most diehard partisans of the ruling parties.

No aim of national revival can ignore the need for urgent changes which will eliminate the most damaging abuses of present government. Such changes call not merely for a new type of political party but entirely new types of men to take over the nation's destinies.

We have got to create new standards of leadership and a new appreciation of the duties of government.

We want a government of the nation, which is not linked to the interests of any particular social class; we need a higher level of political life on which great questions are determined according to the principles of statesmanship rather than by the voice of the mob; we need government with the will to get the things done that have to be done if we are to make our way as a modern nation.

Let us briefly consider a few aspects in which leadership has been utterly lacking in Britain in recent times.

No-one needs telling that our country today is suffering from mounting anarchy and disorder. Universities have capitulated to the rule of a revolutionary rabble. Our city streets have become the scenes of the most violent demonstrations, with the Police asked to bear an intolerable strain which increasingly diverts their manpower from the task of tackling normal crime. In Northern Ireland things have developed to the point of civil war.

In the face of this disorder the initiative of government has been pitiable. To begin with, our elected leaders seem to be oblivious to its source. They think, speak and act as if the disorder is spontaneous, owing its existence to nothing more than the normal tensions within society and the normal protest of youth. They appear to have no conception of the fact that disorder is being deliberately promoted on an international scale and from an international source, employing vast funds of money and the most sophisticated revolutionary techniques; that the mobsters on the streets, whether they be in Belfast or Grosvenor Square, are nothing more than the minor stooges of an immense worldwide organisation for subversion and insurrection.

As the source is not recognised, neither is the source tackled. Disorder is dealt with purely on the spot, after it happens and then always inadequately because there simply are not enough police to go round. The Police do a magnificent job — within the limits of their strength and of the powers given to them, but the fact remains that for every mobster that is caught and punished (lightly of course) there are fifty that get away with it.

And today we have reached a state where the mobsters have so much taken over that government cannot decide whether to confine them or the law-abiding citizens that are their victims. When a minority of extreme left-wing thugs threatened to disrupt by violent means the most ancient and peaceful British custom of playing test cricket, whom did the Labour Government order to desist from their activities? Not the thugs but the people playing cricket! And Tory Government so far has shown itself to be little better. When the perfectly peaceful and legal march of the Orangemen in Ulster was threatened with counter-demonstrations calculated to develop into violent attacks, instead of banning the counter-demonstrations it tried to put pressure on the Orangemen to call their march off. Fortunately, the pressure failed.

With such a conception of the duties of government, how can it be a surprise that there is a declining respect for government?

Responsible and enlightened government would of course tackle violence and disorder at its roots — by penetrating to the heart of the organisations that plan it and acting against those organisations according to the ethics of war which are the only ethics that they themselves recognise. This has nothing to do with the suppression of lawful dissent or protest, only the suppression of those bodies and individuals that by organisation, training and incitement ensure that protest will be used as a pretext for civil disorder and violence.

Every government in history that has failed to act firmly and ruthlessly against the forces of violence and insurrection has sooner or later succumbed to violence and insurrection.

The same criminal neglect of government responsibility can be seen in the failure to act against anarchy in industry, with disastrous results to our economic well being.

Volumes have been written about the reforms necessary to restore harmony and peace to British industry to the point where there is absolutely no lack of formulae, and it is not the purpose here to add more — if it were possible to add more — to what has already been put on record. It is sufficient to say that government, whether of the left or the right, has had ample data and ideas upon which to act — but has not so far acted because the will and the character has not been there to do so.

Naturally, action in this field, as in the field of disorderly demonstrations involves treading on toes. But let us understand whose toes. Just as firm action against violent demonstrators does not infringe upon the right of protest and dissent but purely on the rights of certain subversive bodies to turn that protest and dissent towards their own revolutionary ends, firm action to penalise industrial disruption does not infringe upon the right of workers to freely negotiate wage-agreements but only upon the entrenched privilege of union bosses to bring the economy to a halt at any time that it suits their political purposes to do so.

Responsible national leadership would have acted a long time ago to press through all the reforms needed to make our system of industrial relations as modern and efficient as any in the world, calling the bluff of left-wing union bandits and ignoring the whines and screams of the liberal press. And able national leadership would at the same time have persuaded the mass of workers that such action was as much in their interests as that of their employers. But neither qualities have been shown and industry continues to lurch along governed by the methods and attitudes of the Nineteenth Century.

The refusal of successive governments to act firmly against disorder, as against industrial anarchy and ordinary crime, is very largely the result of a hypnosis created by the opinion media, which in these times have become the almost complete monopoly of permissive liberals.

More will be said later of the obnoxious influence of the media. What must be said here is that one national leader after another in modern times seems to have succumbed to a kind of paralysis of mind and will as a result of paying too much attention to the media and thereby obtaining a picture of national consensus that is likely to be totally distorted. The judgement that every politician brings to an issue today is two-dimensional: one voice within him asks "what is the right thing to do from the standpoint of the national interest?" Another asks "what is the course most likely to be well received by the opinion-forming elite, on whose support my position depends?" It is the second voice which today is heeded the most, but in fact what we need are political leaders who will be guided entirely by the first. Real leadership does not frame its actions to court popularity; it acts according to its own judgement and then wins a measure of popularity first by persuading others that the action is right and finally proving by events that it is right. It is this leadership that we need today, but this leadership of which today we have almost none.

And there is another feature to this mentality: the belief that actions must bow to the mythical altar of 'world opinion'. Here the results for Britain have been catastrophic.

We have heard quoted to excess the Johnsonian assertion that "patriotism is the last refuge of a scoundrel". Far more applicable to our times would be the statement that 'world opinion' is the last refuge of a traitor — and indeed of every doctrinaire internationalist who would jeopardise the interests of his country. In three particular fields of policy, ultimately related, our leaders have made 'world opinion' a ridiculous sacred cow. The first is in the matter of our relations with South Africa and Rhodesia, two countries that are our firm and loyal friends. We have betrayed this friendship at enormous cost to ourselves in trade and world power largely to appease 'world opinion' in the form of a cacophony of agitation from the Afro-Asian bloc. In the same cause of appeasement, and of the same bloc, we have shirked the duty of immigration control in Britain for far too long. Finally, for the same reasons again we have surrendered to the superstition that it is the solemn moral obligation of the advanced countries of the world to give away a portion of their hard-gotten wealth every year to the backward and the ill-governed.

It is bad enough that our politicians actions are so much dictated by 'world opinion' in any shape or form; it is ten times worse that they are compelled by that very section of world opinion that is the least enlightened and most bigoted and which on the basis of true weight of power has the very least right to be listened to.

What we need in the future is a breed of statesman who will follow what his conscience knows to be right for Britain and for the British people and when 'world opinion' objects to tell it in no uncertain terms where to go!

Another characteristic of government in Britain for many decades now has been the utter incapacity to think and act in the long term — in the interests of posterity. Mr Heath, in his speeches during the 1970 Election, talked of policies being framed 'towards the long term', but in practice there is not the slightest sign that his party is any the more influenced by truly long term considerations than Labour; on the contrary, there is every sign that its concern is purely for its month to month electoral prospects and its rating in the now mostly discredited opinion polls.

By the phrase 'long term' we must understand of course a way of thinking and planning that puts priority upon the fundamental needs of national survival, not only in coming decades but indeed in coming centuries.

Policies conceived from this point of view would consider first of all the need for the British people to acquire and control resources which would provide adequate nourishment for scores of unborn generations without all the environmental evils of a crowded, polluted urban existence such as we have today and without the unhealthy attendant necessities such as population control, which if followed to conclusion will keep our numbers down while other nations in the world, not all of them friendly, are expanding at an enormous rate. Such policies would call for a provision for the dispersal of the British race on a vast scale into the open spaces of the Commonwealth so as to develop the resources of the latter to the very full for our own ends. They would be encouraged to live off the land they have settled and to sustain large and vigorous agrarian communities instead of all moving in hordes into the cities. When these things are considered it will be seen that previous British Governments have not been too much imperialist but not nearly imperialist enough. Now with the old imperial structure destroyed, it is nevertheless vital to pursue within the new Commonwealth structure the same kind of development, but nowhere in the thinking of the old parties and the old type leadership is there even the beginning of a recognition of such needs.

Right now discussion of environmental problems such as city crowding and pollution has become a fashionable thing, and so-called 'experts' representing many nations are frenziedly convening together debating this theme with all the self-importance of men who have suddenly hit upon a newly discovered truth. In fact from Britain's point of view the problem should have been seen many decades ago as an endemic result of our chosen path of economic development. Wise economic and geopolitical policies determined upon and firmly put into action then would have averted the present misery, but no such policies were forthcoming. Thinking in the long term was not, and is not, a British political habit. Now we wilt under the problems of our modern environment as if they were a phenomenon that has suddenly descended upon us through an unkind whim of the gods. The foresight of earlier generations of political leadership could in fact have spared us these problems or at least handed them down to us in greatly lightened form. The foresight of a new generation of leadership can lighten them to an extent within our lifetime and perhaps save posterity from them altogether.

The same concern for long term survival would be reflected in many other fields, such as the flat-out development of the depressed areas of Britain itself and the halting of population movement away from them, an intensive programme for a modern motorway system, far greater afforestation, development of greater agricultural self-sufficiency from a strategic as well as an economic point of view, town planning which would consider traffic needs generations ahead instead of just a few years ahead. In these and any number of other spheres government thinking has either been non-existent completely or just tuned to the short space of time that exists between winning one election and fighting the next. Far-sighted planning has been ceaselessly sacrificed for quick profit and expediency,

In no department has this shortcoming been more dangerously manifest than in national defence. Each successive government has made a political virtue out of economies in defence spending and has accepted as axiomatic that the latter should be adapted to the national budget — whereas in truth the reverse should be the case; It is quite appalling that a party that lays claim to about half the nation's votes and is liable under present circumstances to be in power about half the time should believe as a basic element of its philosophy that strong military preparedness is an archaic concept fit only for the support of upper class blimps and romantics — instead of being a fundamental national necessity accepted by all classes alike. But it is hardly less appalling that the party with a claim to the support of the other half of the population and which is in power the other half of the time should be so prepared to compromise with such a philosophy and to so readily act against its inner conscience in order to avoid the troublesome reality that modem military power is as necessary to Britain as it ever was and that modern military power costs a great deal of money.

An escape route from this reality is of course sought by the politicians who seek to make good the shortcomings in Britain's defences by reliance upon such concepts as 'interdependence' and 'collective security'. But this kind of policy rests upon an absurd supposition that existing world alignments are fixed and permanent and indeed on the accompanying supposition that those with whom we are aligned will necessarily die for our interests in any and every contingency. In truth, while there is a place for international alliances in every defensive scheme, that place should never be exaggerated, and it becomes dangerously exaggerated when it embraces reliance on foreign factories for the most basic items of contemporary weapon power.

If there is to be a return to fully responsible government in this country it must include a willingness to commit the national budget to the very fullest defence expenditure that national security demands, and furthermore to recognise national security as meaningless so long as it does not include the capacity to maintain itself entirely from the nation's own industrial and technological resources.

These then are a few of the requirements of government if it is to be considered fit to lead. But government in Britain also has to function under the terms of British democracy, or at least if it does not it has no right to claim treatment under those terms. And government cannot function under the terms of democracy while on great fundamental issues it functions in contempt of a large part of the electorate.

In recent years the issues of the Common Market, immigration and several spheres of permissive law-making, notably capital punishment and abortion, have provided glaring examples of government by consensus of a liberal minority and without the remotest mandate from the population as a whole. It is a complete mockery of the term 'democratic' to permit government to be carried on in this way.

No serious person would suggest that the Government ask the permission of the electorate before every minor day to day decision is made; that would not be government at all, since such decisions call for an expertise that the electorate as a whole simply does not possess. But government, and in particular government resting on democratic foundations, is treading on highly dangerous ground when without any indication of popular consent it becomes committed to policies that involve changes in the nation's entire way of life and in the entire foundations of its existence. Government under these terms has become a modern habit, and as such has no right whatever to be judged according to the ethos of democracy.

Not only do we in this country need strong and responsible government, we have a right to demand at the same time that it is representative government, and to be that it must in some way establish mandate from the electorate in all issues where a crossroads has been reached in national destinies.

If the reader has grasped the point of this chapter he will gather that Nationalists seek a type of government with a firmness and strength that we have not seen in this country for at least half a century, but at the same time a government that acts within the democratic terms on which it has been elected. Firmness and strength can more easily be exercised within a dictatorship; within a democracy of the British character they call for leadership of a very high order. Persuasion rather than suppression must be the usual practice.

If we are not to have dictatorship, what we certainly do need is a governing party that can gain an ascendency in British politics of sufficient dimensions, and for a sufficient period of time, to attend to vital tasks uninterrupted until they have become part of the permanent pattern of British life. How is this to be done?

There seems little likelihood of it being done with the present political balance as even as it is. The assertion that the two leading parties can lay claim to roughly two halves of the nation's votes is more or less true—at least in respect of habitual and ingrained loyalties. The balance at each election is, as we know, tipped by the floating voter who never comes to shore long enough to give any government worthwhile security of tenure. It is perhaps hardly surprising that the floating disease eventually affects government as well.

To get away from floating voter politics effectively and permanently we require one leading party to be able, in addition to retaining its own traditional elements of support, to make vast inroads into those of the others—in other words, to break the habits of generations and to bring about a complete realignment of voting groups within British society.

Given the character, image and psychology of Conservative and Labour parties, such a prospect seems remote. Long standing class divisions, however irrational, do not appear as if they can be reconciled by the traditional followers of one attaching themselves to the other.

Such a reconciliation could only be achieved by a synthesis of both elements in a new political movement which by tradition was identified neither with one class nor the other; a movement which would truly embody the national unity to which Tory and Labour pay lip service but just cannot somehow achieve themselves.

The old parties cannot bring this about; only a new party can.

This then is the object of Nationalists in Britain: a new party of the character that can capture a majority following from both sides of the present political spectrum so as to be able to obtain a long and assured term of power necessary to its tasks.

# 6. REGENERATION WITHIN

The collapse of mighty nations has been a subject of endless historical analysis to which the most profound intellects of the ages have been applied. Out of the vast subject matter that has been compiled one clear rule stands out: mere material disasters alone, such as economic depression, defeat in war, etc., are not enough. At the most they are effects rather than causes and can only do permanent damage when the product of deeper spiritual and psychological forces that have eaten into national morale and deprived the community of all will to life. When a vigorous and creative people suddenly abdicates all power and loses its capacity to function, when at every crossroads it chooses with mechanical reliability the route that is sure to lead in the opposite direction to that required by its national interests, when it opts to become alienated from its natural friends and to make common cause with its natural enemies, when it pillories its prophets and honours its clowns, when after centuries of spectacular success it staggers from one to another humiliating failure — it is surely pertinent to ask: why does it do these things?

When in 1940 the German Army ran through France to occupy Paris and forced French surrender within the fantastic space of nine weeks, the world asked in astonishment: what has happened to the once great French nation?

Historians are fairly unanimous about the answer. It was not lack of guns that caused the French defeat; it was utter and complete moral disintegration. For several decades authors, playwrights, poets, artists, and political philosophers had run rampant in French society who had undermined all patriotism, sneered at every pillar of national tradition and promoted in the name of 'progress' every imaginable cult of degeneracy. France had become synonymous in the mind of the world with loose morals, male foppishness, 'way-out' trends in art and fashion, indulgent habits and a national obsession with erotica. By the time war had arrived that nation was more than ripe for collapse.

Those who can recall this condition will immediately realise the frightening parallel in present day Britain.

Our theatres and bookshops abound with products of filth and license, spreading contempt for every civilised institution upon which our nation has been built. Marriage, the family, social responsibility, personal restraint, respect for the law, thrift and work: all are derided in favour of the 'new morality' the message of which is: live for the moment! Live on impulse! Live for fun and kicks!

As these influences have served to rot our moral fabric and create a complete vacuum in the way of spiritual belief, into this vacuum have stepped Communists, Anarchists and every other kind of fellow traveller of the Left. Like a relentless insect army they have infiltrated into every compartment of British life, spreading doctrines of subversion, denigrating old loyalties and values and paralysing every healthy expression of the British character.

Their product is an increasing generation of aimless young men and women whose most symbolic activity is that of squatting down in public squares and proclaiming that their country is not worth fighting for. This generation wears its many badges ubiquitously and shamelessly: idleness and exhibitionism, drug addiction and dirt, weediness and effeminacy, hooliganism and nihilism. All these characteristics have come to the fore in Britain today and serve to present an appalling national image in the eyes of the world.

Do the leaders of society deplore these trends? Do they try to use their influence to combat them? Quite the contrary, many seem to want to encourage them. As the crime rate reaches ever higher proportions, we are told that it is a sign of 'enlightenment' to make life increasingly more pleasant for the criminal. As the rate of illegitimacy soars, the answer is not to encourage human restraint but to legalise abortion. As productivity falls further behind the rest of the world, we not only tolerate anarchy in industry but are glad to subsidise a growing horde of workshy humanity which lives comfortably off our public welfare institutions up and down the land.

Indeed, the worst feature of these trends is that they are being consciously promoted, sometimes out of perverted conviction, sometimes for plain commercial profit, by those very elements of society from whom the country has a right to expect the best example. Press and television, as well as the schools and universities, have become the breeding grounds of all those ideas that are systematically rotting the nation from within. These institutions, aided now by large sections of the Clergy, do everything to foster and praise the most obscene tendencies in art, literature, ethics and human behaviour. We are in an age in which we can be sure that everything which is decadent in the national fabric will find its eager throng of sponsors in the highest as well as the lowest strata of the community.

Characteristically, the promoters of this poison claim that it is in keeping with the principle of academic and cultural 'freedom' — the holy phrase by which liberals always seek to justify their onslaught on ordered society. In fact it is becoming increasingly apparent that real freedom is the very last thing of which the liberals approve. Once they have got their clutches on a particular medium through which the public can be influenced, they go all out to exclude any views or ideas that they decide are a threat to their growing hegemony of the mind. As an example of this, why not devote the next few minutes you have to spare in trying to recall the last time a novel was accorded top ratings by the press and TV critics whose hero or heroine did not break at least three of the basic rules of civilised society. You would have to go back no little time. The sponsors of the 'new morality' are quite set on making theirs the only morality. The censorship they oppose is only the censorship of their own products. Once in control, they will be found rigidly censoring the products of others.

This 'permissive society' and all its symptoms are generally associated with the political Left, and it is perfectly true that Fabian intellectuals have done more than most to rationalise permissiveness and the breakdown in the social order that is its consequence. But what of the political 'Right'? What of Conservatism? To say the least, Tories, either when in Government or in Opposition, have shown themselves pitifully apathetic towards the duty of opposing these corrupting tendencies in society. If Tory doctrines and policies be examined, it will be found that nowhere is there even the faintest recognition that Britain is in the throes of a crisis of morale and of social stability which is every bit as great as any political or economic crisis. Responsible national leadership would recognise this crisis and take firm measures to deal with it. Perhaps it is endemic in the psyche of modern Conservatism that it can only recognise a state of emergency in matters that can be judged in terms of pounds, shillings and pence.

Conditions such as these surely point out the prior task facing the future leadership of Britain. Before all else, there must be a complete moral regeneration of the national life, beginning with government and penetrating downwards into every sphere of work and leisure. By 'moral regeneration' let us not mean a return to puritanism or to the absurd inhibitions that formed part of Victorian life but simply to the values of order, responsibility and restraint which are essential to the survival of any social structure and ultimately of any nation.

In such a task not only government but the great opinion media of press and television must play their part.

The first necessity is a clear programme of legislation which will render liable to prosecution all persons or agencies responsible for the promotion of art, literature or entertainment by which public moral standards might be endangered. Quite clearly, the existing laws dealing with obscenity in these fields are inadequate and must be strengthened, as must the penalties for their infringement be made firmer.

Such strengthening of the law should be quite enough to cause the closure of the multitude of bookshops, clubs, theatres and other establishments which make money out of the corruption of young minds and by catering for all that is lowest and most depraved in public taste.

These young minds should indeed be our first concern. Why today are they so vulnerable to every kind of poison fed to them by the political propagandists and teachers of license? The answer is not a simple one. When a society becomes so far advanced along the road to demoralisation it becomes more and more difficult to sort out effect from cause. However, certain pointers do indicate lamentable weaknesses in our system of bringing up the young. We are today hypnotised by liberal attitudes which condemn all concepts of strong authority and worship the cult of permissiveness. We therefore lose sight of some of the most essential needs of the younger generation in its preparation for citizenship.

A great furore rages at the present time in our educational world over methods of academic selection, but whilst it would not be right to understate the importance of such issues it seems astonishing that the academic side alone dominates the minds of our educational 'experts'. We hear very little about the training of body and character and the instillation of real values that have been a feature of the public school system but which in fact should permeate all education.

In one element in particular we are lacking today and we pay dearly for it. There is almost no attempt to instil into youth the basic principles of patriotism. These are best developed, not by lengthy repetitions of slogans and paths or a merely mechanical singing of the national anthem every morning, but by a full and vivid teaching of British and Imperial history from the standpoint of national achievement; also by a comprehensive outline of the greatness of the British heritage both in this country and throughout the world and the duties that this imposes on those who accede to it. Better than just saying to youth: you must be loyal to Queen and Country, we should give youth a full picture of what Queen and Country represent, and encourage loyalty and patriotism to spring from that picture by a spontaneous process. It need hardly be said of course that British youth is not likely to be instilled with patriotic pride while living under politicians who seem out to humiliate Britain at every opportunity, and being taught by academics who prefer to give the Marxist interpretation of British history as a saga of guilt and shame. New leaders, as well as new teachers, are an essential need before any reform in the trend of education can be expected.

But if and when this elementary need was adopted — as it once was in Britain and as it still is in all strongly organised nations — our young men and women would grow to adulthood much more resistant to the left-wing virus which today is rife throughout the upper echelons of society.

We should not forget that while we are bringing up our younger generations to look at the world from an internationalist, pacifistic point of view there are other nations that are imbuing their young with a strident and aggressive nationalism. In future issues of survival this will not work to our advantage.

Aside from this, we need to promote in the young much more than we do at present the ideal of physical health and fitness. Healthy thoughts flow from a healthy being, and it is no coincidence that the large number of overpampered, physically effete half-men that we seem to be turning out nowadays are the most vulnerable to the many poisons that are seductively offered in the darker corners of the big city. Cultivate in a young man's mind the idea of sound physical health as a permanent obligation to himself, his country, his creator and, not least, the offspring that he is going to bring into the world; cultivate in him the joyful self-confidence of being a physically whole person; and cultivate in him the physical capacity for hard work and great efforts of the will; cultivate these things, and add to them a strong sense of patriotism and the social consciousness that stems from it, and you will breed a type of far greater value to Britain than the now all too common species of walking greenhouse-flower.

Apologists for this type of 'flower generation' insist that it is only, conforming to a passing fashion, presumably with reference to styles of hair and clothing. But this is missing the point. The public revulsion to the type which one senses amongst most normal people is primarily against the man, or lack of it, that is underneath the hair and inside - the clothes. True enough, Elizabethan man wore his hair long and his clothes decorative, but there the resemblance ends. Study the firm features and erect bearing of men of that period and compare them with the pallid, vacuous look and slouching deportment of these latter-day specimens, and the point may then be better understood. The fashions are a secondary product. What comes first is the personality itself.

In a sound educational system this product would be a rarity. The object of our schools and universities should be to produce complete people. It is the single-minded emphasis on intellect for its own sake, and its resultant tendency to reduce all vital questions of existence down to a flat, uninspired pseudo-rationale, that atrophies the much more potent factors of instinct and will which move great and vigorous races and which ultimately determine history.

As a final point, something should be said about the institution of national service. We had national service in Britain until a few years ago, when a Tory Government calculated that it would purchase votes by abolishing it. Most other powers still have it.

Dangerous unpreparedness in two world wars should have convinced us of the necessity of a universal period of military service for young men purely from the standpoint of national defence and security. However, we are concerned here less with the strategic aspect than with the beneficial effect of such an institution on all men who pass through it. Beyond any doubt, the back-straightening influence of service life, with its emphasis on smartness and discipline and the values of manhood, made men better fitted altogether, not only for the emergencies of war, but also for the everyday tasks of peace. The return of this institution, possibly combined with labour service in great public works, could be an incalculable boon to Britain, and its costs could be more than justified by the long term effects on the fitness and morale of the population.

These three factors: patriotic education, sound health and service training, do not solve every moral and social problem with which we are beset, but they do breed a sturdier race, better equipped to cope with the challenges of life and better fortified against its harmful influences.

These factors considered, what of the role of press, television and similar institutions? Today it is impossible to estimate the enormous influence that these media have on the whole range of popular attitudes. They are to an overwhelming extent the setters of fashion, the creators of taste, the moulders of thought and the models for behaviour. Their influence can be used, as at present, to undermine and rot the nation's moral fibre, or to strengthen and uplift it.

Obviously, we want the latter.

The opinion media, both in Britain and elsewhere in the world where they exercise much the same influence, are of course passionately jealous of their privileges and rights. This was made clear by their outraged reaction to the statement by US Vice President Agnew that some of them were abusing their power. They immediately protested to the heavens about the dangers of their being 'gagged'. But in fact they were simply sidetracking the issue. They themselves are the most accomplished exponents of the art of 'gagging' views that they do not favour and boycotting by silence politicians they dislike and fear. Most of the criticism of the opinion media today comes, not from people who want to 'gag' them, but only from those who want to see them fulfil their assumed role as truly democratic institutions for the really free expression of views and ideas and for the representation of the 'silent majority' as well as the vociferous intellectual minority. At the same time it is surely reasonable to ask that the opinion media recognise some kind of responsibility for the maintaining of decency and good morale among the population, particularly the impressionable younger population.

With regard to the BBC in particular, it should be realised that this is a public corporation sustained by licence payers money and as such has a firm duty to those licence-payers to carry out their wishes with regard to programmes where questions of public decency are involved as well as to see that a balance of political viewpoints is maintained.

In the mass media we have in our hands an instrument which, if properly used, could serve to ennoble our whole national life. It is a criminal folly that we have allowed this instrument to be used for the very opposite purpose.

Aside from the factors that have been examined, there is another institution that has had an appalling effect on Britain in the standards it, has set and the attitudes it has bred. This is our current form of welfare state and its scale of social benefits. Today this institution thwarts every effort to get Britain moving into the Twentieth Century.

The governing slogan of our welfare state today is the classical bolshevik one: "To each according to his needs". In effect this means that every drone, sponger and drop-out can be kept comfortably at the expense of honest and industrious folk — providing that he can prove such 'needs' to his local welfare officer. The result is a growing army of the parasitic and the workshy, perfectly able-bodied but just not interested in any useful employment whatsoever so long as it is possible to draw a generous loafer's allowance from the State. To keep this army satisfied and well cared for we have to add hugely to our public expenditure, which in turn causes an endless rise in taxation. Typically, successive governments have placed the main burden of this rise on the higher income groups, which of course are less numerous and from whom therefore less votes can be lost. The outcome is that an ever greater number of our most capable and ambitious men leave us and go abroad with the same depressing tale: "There is no incentive to work hard and get on in this country anymore; the more you earn, the more they take away from you". The best are penalised for their efforts in order that the worst may be rewarded for their laziness. Is it any wonder that our national standards decline — so long as we punish ability and encourage lead-swinging?

To remedy this condition we need a complete change in our welfare system and its scale of rewards and social benefits. Instead of the slogan "To each according to his needs", our principle should be: "To each according to his desserts". Let people get out of the nation precisely what they put into it. Let social security be commensurate with the useful effort that the worker contributes to the prosperity of the nation. Let those who work hard, study, train, save and develop their skills be amply rewarded and encouraged to improve themselves still more. Let those who prefer the life of slothful ease suffer for it by hardship, shortage and insecurity until they decide to mend their ways.

This does not mean that social benefits should be withheld from those whose needs are due to ordinary misfortune or to economic factors outside their control; quite the contrary. But it does mean that we should exercise much more discrimination in sorting out the genuinely unfortunate from those who are simply out to use the welfare state as a substitute for honest toil.

Basically, we need to depart radically from the leftist philosophy which holds that the nation owes everyone a living, and to develop a social welfare system which encourages to the utmost the principles of hard work, self-reliance and personal responsibility. By setting these principles in the forefront of our thinking we will lay the foundation stones of a prosperous and vigorous national community.

Will Britain in the years to come grasp and apply these things in a determined effort to renew and revitalise herself within? Will this nation whose peerless record of achievement has enriched every corner of the globe and whose fighting spirit has proved unconquerable for so long challenge and overcome the most deadly foe of all—the sickness within herself? This is the dominating question of our times, and beside it the doctrinaire disputes of parliamentary parties fade into irrelevancy.

Political policy means nothing if not the nourishment of those inner sinews of life and strength that sustain a nation through the cycles of infinite time, securing the existence of its unborn generations and passing on to them intact the accumulated heritage of all its former struggles and endeavours.

The life sinews of British nationhood lie, as with all others, not in the ephemeral balances of commercial and diplomatic fortune, not in the day to day gains and losses over which current political factions raise steam, but in the moral fibre of Britons themselves, both individually and as a group, in their capacity to create and build, in their readiness to lead and serve, in their will to live as befits a great race.

This inner moral health and strength is more fundamental to our future as a people than any other national issue of the moment. It is central to all politics and transcends all ideology.

Its restoration and sustenance is the crucial task of our leadership now and at all times hence. In an age of challenges the magnitude of which mankind has never before known, let us be fit to stay out in front and win for ourselves a golden stake in the world that is to come.

# Addenda

John Tyndall was born Exeter, 1934. Educated Beckenham Grammar School. Played cricket (School 1st XI and Kent trialist), rugby and soccer (Kent Minor XI). Served in Royal Horse Artillery 1952-54. Began political study and activity soon after leaving forces but did not join any of the older political parties, being convinced that none of them offered the right solutions to Britain's problems. Was active in a number of patriotic and Nationalist groups, including the League of Empire Loyalists, before founding the Greater Britain Movement in 1964 and his own publishing company, Albion Press, and the magazine Spearhead at the same time. He disbanded the GBM in 1967 and with his colleagues joined the National Front. Hobbies: reading, sport and music.

John Hutchyns Tyndall (14 July 1934 - 19 July 2005).

# Postscript to 2nd Edition

Since the first edition of this booklet was published there has arisen for the first time in post-war years a really strong political organisation embracing all the main ideals of British Nationalism. In 1966 a number of nationalist bodies amalgamated together to form the National Front. Since then this movement has absorbed further groups and grown to the stage where it is beyond doubt the most formidable and promising force for Nationalism in Britain today. While, as stated earlier, this booklet represents an individual view, I recommend without hesitation that all those in broad agreement with the ideas set out here join the National Front and give it all the support within their power. Amid the dismal panorama of contemporary British politics, it is the one great hope for the future of this nation.

**JOHN TYNDALL, London, 1970.**

# About The A.K. Chesterton Trust

*The A.K. Chesterton Trust* was formed by Colin Todd and the late Miss. Rosine de Bounevialle in January 1996 to succeed and continue the work of the now defunct Candour Publishing Co.

The objects of the Trust are stated as follows:

**"To promote and expound the principles of A.K. Chesterton which are defined as being to demonstrate the power of, and to combat the power of International Finance, and to promote the National Sovereignty of the British World."**

Our aims include:

- *Maintaining and expanding the range of material relevant to A.K. Chesterton and his associates throughout his life.*

- *To preserve and keep in-print important works on British Nationalism in order to educate the current generation of our people.*

- *The maintenance and recovery of the sovereign independence of the British Peoples throughout the world.*

- *The strengthening of the spiritual and material bonds between the British Peoples throughout the world.*

- *The resurgence at home and abroad of the British spirit.*

We will raise funds by way of merchandising and donations.

We ask that our friends make provision for *The A.K. Chesterton Trust* in their will.

The A.K. Chesterton Trust has a **duty** to keep *Candour* in the ring and punching.

**CANDOUR: To defend national sovereignty against the menace of international finance.**

**CANDOUR: To serve as a link between Britons all over the world in protest against the surrender of their world heritage.**

# Subscribe to Candour

**CANDOUR SUBSCRIPTION RATES FOR 10 ISSUES.**

U.K. £25.00
Europe 40 Euros.
Rest of the World £35.00.
USA $50.00.

All Airmail. Cheques and Postal Orders, £'s Sterling only, made payable to *The A.K. Chesterton Trust*. (Others, please send cash by **secure post**, $ bills or Euro notes.)

Payment by Paypal is available. Please see our website **www.candour.org.uk** for more information.

# Candour Back Issues

**Back issues are available. 1953 to the present.**

Please request our back issue catalogue by sending your name and address with two 1st class stamps to:

**The A.K. Chesterton Trust, BM Candour, London, WC1N 3XX, UK**

Alternatively, see our website at **www.candour.org.uk** where you can order a growing selection on-line.

# The A.K. Chesterton Trust Reprint Series

1. Creed of a Fascist Revolutionary & Why I Left Mosley - A.K. Chesterton.

2. The Menace of World Government & Britain's Graveyard - A.K. Chesterton.

3. What You Should Know About The United Nations - The League of Empire Loyalists.

4. The Menace of the Money-Power - A.K. Chesterton.

5. The Case for Economic Nationalism - John Tyndall.

6. Sound the Alarm! - A.K. Chesterton.

7. Six Principles of British Nationalism - John Tyndall.

8. B.B.C. - A National Menace - A.K. Chesterton

9. Stand By The Empire - A.K. Chesterton

10. Tomorrow. A Plan for the British Future - A.K. Chesterton.

11. The British Constitution and the Corruption of Parliament - Ben Greene.

12. Very High Finance & The Policy of a Patriot - Cahill & Strasser

# Other Titles from The A.K. Chesterton Trust

Leopard Valley - A.K. Chesterton

Juma The Great - A.K. Chesterton

The New Unhappy Lords - A.K. Chesterton

Facing The Abyss - A.K. Chesterton

The History of the League of Empire Loyalists - McNeile & Black

Common Market Suicide – A.K. Chesterton

The Candour A.B.C. of Politics – Rosine de Bounevialle

Hidden Government – J Creagh-Scott

**All the above titles are available from The A.K. Chesterton Trust, BM Candour, London, WC1N 3XX, UK**

**www.candour.org.uk**

Printed in Great Britain
by Amazon